THEY DIED TOO YOUNG

MARILYN MONROE

BY
Esther Selsdon

This edition first published by Parragon Books Ltd in 1995

Produced by
Magpie Books Ltd, London

Unit 13–17, Avonbridge Trading Estate
Atlantic Road
Avonmouth
Bristol BS11 9QD

Illustrations courtesy of: Rex Features

ISBN 0 75250 700 1

A copy of the British Library Cataloguing in Publication Data is available from the British Library.

Typeset by Hewer Text Composition Services, Edinburgh
Printed in Singapore by Printlink International Co.

THEY DIED TOO YOUNG
Marilyn Monroe

Early Years

In 1899 Della Mae Hogan, having earlier scandalized her local Missouri community by encouraging local lads to play 'kiss-me-quick' in a variety of neighbourhood farmyards, came to her senses and married a house painter, ten years her senior, called Otis Elmer Monroe. Just a few months later, Otis, who had high hopes of becoming a famous artist and moving to Paris, France, took his wife across the border to Mexico, where he was sure that they would save enough money to facilitate their trip to Europe. Instead, in 1902, Della gave birth to a girl, Gladys Pearl, and the Monroes, with their lofty dreams fading, moved to Los Angeles where they had heard that the trams, if not the streets, needed covering in gold. In 1905, Della gave birth to a boy called Marion. Work became scarcer and Otis began to drink.

By 1908 Otis was semi-paralysed. He was in the final stages of syphilis of the brain, and the cure was not to be invented for another year – which was too late to save Otis. He died in 1909 at the age of forty-three. Otis's deterioration had been rapid and terrifying – Della was convinced that her husband had gone mad. In fact, the kind of syphilis from which he suffered was not hereditary and nor was it sexually contracted. He had almost certainly caught it working in the unhygienic conditions prevalent at that time in Mexico. Still, Della brought up her children to believe that their father had perished horribly, riddled with insanity, and the whole family was convinced.

Della rapidly remarried but her second husband also took to drink and she, just as swiftly, left him. By the end of 1916 she had moved with her children to the Venice Beach area of Santa Monica, south of Los Angeles, at which time Gladys was fourteen and her brother, Marion, eleven. Della believed that boys should have a father-figure and sent

Marion to live with some cousins in San Diego. She then rapidly found a new boyfriend who wished her to cohabit without the encumbrance of a teenage daughter. Simultaneously, Gladys met a twenty-six-year-old Kentucky businessman called John Baker who was smitten with the child. Della cheerfully falsified her daughter's age, witnessed the marriage and moved in with her boyfriend.

At first, Gladys was quite happy. The couple had two children, Jack and Berniece, and things looked rosy. But Gladys had never known family life and quickly grew bored with motherhood. She began to leave her children in the care of neighbours and spend her time out dancing, whilst her husband worked long hours as a travelling salesman. By

1921 she had had enough of this particular life and so she simply filed for a new one. Though Baker did not contest the divorce, he was a responsible father and, when the annulment came through, he upped and left California, taking both of his children back with him to Kentucky. Gladys went to visit them once, about a year later, and that was that. She was glad that they were gone and that she could get on with the serious business of life – having fun.

She got a job as a splicer of negative film stock in the newly-developing film industry and she became friends with another regular party-lover, Grace McKee. By the end of 1923 Grace and Gladys were flatmates in Hollywood and, as far as Gladys was concerned, real life had begun. Grace was twenty-eight and already married three times, without having bothered to divorce the first two husbands. Grace and Gladys were fast-living women. They were keen to emulate the lives of the glamorous stars, thousands of whose images passed before their cutting-machines every day at work. Under Grace's groovy influence, Gladys dyed her hair cherry-red and, immediately, she was transformed.

Gladys started dating a Norwegian meterman called Martin Edward Mortensen. He asked her to marry him. It was October 1924. He was five years older than her, he was good-looking and he had a rather dashing facial scar. She had no reason to say 'no'. Four months later,

Gladys, following in her mother's footsteps, simply got bored with her second husband and moved back in with Grace. Ten months later she discovered she was pregnant. She went to her mother, who was busy making plans to travel abroad with her boyfriend and took no interest in the matter. Gladys was on her own.

The baby was born on 1 June 1926 at 9.30 a.m. in the Los Angeles General Hospital and the birth certificate identifies her as the daughter of Gladys Monroe of Wilshire Boulevard. Gladys simply claimed that her first two children had died and, as for the father, she designated her husband, Edward Mortenson, residence unknown. The baby was registered as Norma Jeane Mortenson, though she might well have been the offspring of any number of men. In 1925, Gladys was going out with her foreman, a married man called Charles Gifford, two co-workers, Harold Rooney and Clayton MacNamara; and a film developer called Raymond Guthrie. She wasn't bothered as to the paternity of the child and neither were they. Norma Talmadge was Gladys's favourite film star at the time and that was about as far as their combined interest went. Within two weeks, Gladys had given Norma Jeane to a foster family, sixteen miles away.

Ida and Albert Bolender were religious people who made extra money by taking in foster children, for whose care they were paid twenty-five dollars a month by the State of California. A year later, Della became ill with breathing and heart problems. She was convinced that death was near and, with difficulty, struggled over to the Bolenders to see her only proximate grandchild. Breaking the door with her elbow, she demanded entry. Thinking she was a burglar, the Bolenders called the police. Della was arrested and carted away to the hospital. She died soon afterwards of heart disease, but the myth of family insanity deepened.

Norma Jeane stayed with the Bolenders for seven years. Life in their house was rigidly disciplined and ruthlessly authoritarian. She washed every day and went to church several times a week. Dancing, drinking and, particularly, moviegoing were considered works of the devil. The most hedonistic interlude for Norma Jeane was the acquisition of a dog called Tippy. She was a withdrawn child and he was the only creature to whom she spoke. She made no friends. And then, quite suddenly, with the irresponsible whimsy to which she had been prone her whole life, Gladys, hearing that Tippy had died, came to collect Norma Jeane and take her back to a home she had never known. The child was seven years old.

They shared a house with Grace and a couple of English part-time actors. Norma Jeane, who had scarcely ever seen her mother, was disoriented and confused. 'Aunt Ida is not my mother,' she told herself. 'The lady with the red hair is my mother.' The lady with the red hair, however, was about as different from any notion Norma had of motherhood as one could imagine. Gladys went to movies and had boyfriends and drank beer. Gladys even took her to the movies and actually admired the brazen hussy, Jean Harlow. The world was an astonishing mixture of influences for the seven-year-old Norma. A strange and confusing place.

That autumn, Gladys, who had never known her grandfather, received the news that, following the Great Depression and his own bankruptcy, he had hanged himself. Though, in reality, this was just another of the thousands of suicides recorded that year, Gladys fell into a stupefied depression. She now considered that both of her parents

An early modelling shot of Norma Jeane

Marilyn Monroe

and her grandfather had died of madness and she was not to be dissuaded. She stalked the house, reading out loud from the Bible and wept continually. After several weeks Grace called in the neurologist, who gave Gladys some pills to which she had a violent reaction. In modern terms, Gladys was suffering from depression; but this was not understood at the time and she was taken to a rest home, where heavy sedation took its toll on her health. Gradually she ceased to speak or to communicate with the outside world. It was now Grace's turn to play mother.

Where Gladys had merely lived a life of fun, Grace positively embraced it. With Norma Jeane she indulged all of her wildest motherhood fantasies, dressing her up in gingham, curling her hair and assuring her that she would, one day, be a big movie star. She insisted that a friend fetch Norma to the film lab an hour before closing every Saturday, and then she would make the child walk up and down and say repeatedly, 'I'm going to be a movie star'. This charade continued every week for months and months and, since Jean Harlow was Grace's favourite star, Jean Harlow was to be the model for emulation. Norma Jeane's fate was sealed.

Grace decided to become Norma's legal guardian, but the State of California required proof that the living parents were incompetent or dead. Grace easily obtained a formal statement from doctors that Gladys was insane and, after her condition stabilized, the General Hospital said that it could no longer accommodate her. She was sent to a psychiatric hospital where she eventually died. On 1 June 1935, Grace McKee took full possession of everything that Gladys Baker owned and, at long last, it seemed that Norma Jeane might find a stable home environment.

And then Ervin Silliman Goddard appeared. He was ten years younger than Grace and was Joel McCrea's stand-in on movies. Grace, who had decided to focus all of her life's interests on Norma Jeane, suddenly developed some new ones of her own. She was besotted and the pair married In August, bringing one of 'Doc' Goddard's three daughters back to Los Angeles with them. Grace told

Norma Jeane that there was no room at the inn – Doc's daughter was to have her room and she was to go to an orphanage. And so, on 13 September 1935, Norma Jeane was packed off to the Los Angeles Orphans Home in Hollywood, where she became occupant number 3,463. She stayed there for almost two years, sharing a room with three other girls in conditions which were, generally speaking, acceptable if loveless. Grace frequently appeared on Sundays and took Norma Jeane to a film. She also fixed her hair and gave the girl make-up. These were fantastic treats in an otherwise dreary landscape. She once wrote herself a postcard, signing it from Mummy and Daddy, but the other occupants of the orphanage merely laughed at her folly.

Eventually, a week after her eleventh birthday, Grace lived up to her word. She came to fetch Norma Jeane and take her home, but temporary domesticity was not to last long. Doc Goddard, who had taken to drink, grabbed Norma Jeane one night and, unsuccessfully, tried to molest her. Grace immediately shipped the girl off to board with relatives. 'It was all very confusing,' said Norma Jeane.

From November 1937 to August 1938, Norma Jeane lived about twenty-five miles south-east of Los Angeles, with the mother of Olive Brunings, who had married Gladys's younger brother Marion in 1924. Not surprisingly, given the family history, he had long since disappeared, leaving a household of abandoned children behind him. One of these was a son called Jack who attempted to assault Norma Jeane shortly after her twelfth birthday and, once again, Grace, suddenly and unexpectedly, intervened. She took the child back to Los Angeles to live with her aunt, Ana Lower, a rather well-off, devoutly Christian divorcee. She was the first woman who had ever really cared for Norma Jeane, but Ana was always bitter about her husband's desertion and, in this way, yet another negative female influence on the girl.

Norma Jeane started at the local junior high school, where she was an average pupil. She was embarrassed to wear the same clothes every day and had no idea how to make friends. Norma Jeane, however, was resourceful. She bought a pair of boy's trousers and was the first girl in the class to wear a back-to-front cardigan. Suddenly life seemed full of potential. Every young fellow honked his horn and, for the first time in her life, she was noticed. It was as easy as that. The secret was tight clothing; and now that Norma Jeane knew the secret, she wouldn't forget it in a hurry.

In 1940 Aunt Ana began to suffer from heart problems and Norma Jeane returned to the Goddards, who had, in the meantime, acquired new neighbours with a rather dashing son. Jim Dougherty worked at Lockheed Aircraft and, in 1941, when he met Norma Jeane, was employed as a driver along with another beefy fellow called Robert Mitchum.

Since he had to drive to work every morning, Grace asked him to drop Norma Jeane off at her high school on the way. Jim looked both old and distinguished to his passenger and, displaying the beginnings of a lifetime fixation with older men, she came home to tell her 'cousin' Bebe Goddard that Jim was a 'dreamboat and what a daddy!' Early in 1942, Doc Goddard was told that he was being transferred to West Virginia. Norma Jeane was not to accompany the family and she was told that this was the case. Her respect for Grace dropped dramatically and, in this way, the two women's desires collided. Norma Jeane wanted to leave and Grace wanted her to go. Jim was clearly the answer.

On set at Twentieth-Century Fox

Always the performer

Jim said he agreed to the marriage because he was going into the army anyway and she was a cute little kid. Norma Jeane, still only fifteen, didn't want to go back to the orphanage. In mid-March, two days after the Goddards left for West Virginia, Norma Jeane shocked her teachers by telling them that she leaving to get married in June. This abortive education was to leave her with a permanent inferiority complex. On 1 June 1942 she turned sixteen and, on the 19th, she was married. Norma Jeane was shaking like a leaf and had to be supported. Jim was suffering from the effects of whisky. His wife looked unhappy and she was. They moved into their new, one-room home that same afternoon.

Hollywood Beckons

'She was so sensitive and insecure, I realized I wasn't prepared to handle her,' said Jim. 'She thought I was mad at her if I didn't kiss her goodbye every time I left the house. When we had an argument, I'd often go to sleep on the couch. An hour later, I woke up to find her sleeping alongside me, or sitting nearby on the floor . . . she was very forgiving . . . she never held a grudge in her life.'

Norma Jeane knew nothing about housekeeping or lovemaking and very little about making conversation or friends. She stayed at home and talked to very few people and then, in spring 1944, Dougherty was called up for military service and Norma Jeane begged him not to go. Of course he had to and his wife went to live with her mother-in-law in North Hollywood. She got a job at an aeroplane factory, spraying paint, and it was here that her life suddenly began to change.

The Army's First Motion Picture Unit was sent to the assembly line to photograph women helping with the war effort. Twenty-five-year-old David Conover began taking photographs of Norma Jeane to stunning effect.

Co-operative, eager and bright, she tossed her curly chestnut hair and seemed to come alive in front of a camera. A woman who had never known how to draw attention to her real self, instinctively seemed to know how to flirt with a composed image of herself. Ethel Dougherty was not amused.

Norma Jeane moved into the basement of Aunt Ana's house and her mother-in-law informed Jim, who wrote to his wife telling her that modelling and housewifery were incompatible. Norma Jeane simply took this to mean that her marriage was dissolved. At David's suggestion, Norma Jeane applied to the Blue Book model agency and her first assignment was as a hostess at a first-class hotel.

Ms Sniveley, who ran the agency, was later to say that she didn't think Norma Jeane had ever been inside a hotel before. She was stunned by life's potential opulence. She was enchanted. She would never go back to people like Ethel Dougherty.

By spring 1946 Norma Jeane had appeared on no fewer than thirty-three magazine covers. Sniveley's only recommendation was that Norma should lighten her hair. The model became blonde and, when Jim returned to LA in December 1945, Norma was an hour late to meet him and distinctly cool in her greeting. A few days after his arrival, she left on a modelling shoot with a photographer called Andre de Dienes. 'The truth is', she said, 'that I began the trip with only business in mind. But Andre had other ideas.'

'In my dreams I had explored her body,' reported de Dienes later, 'but reality far surpassed my imagination.' Once initiated into the pleasures of life, Norma Jeane was not only persuaded, she was positively enthusiastic – he was much older; he was handsome and he was a well-known photographer. She returned to LA with a little more savvy and a furious husband. Jim was soon called upon to return to the battlefield and so was she. Over the next few months, she was snapped by large numbers of top photographers and her ambitions became grander. She wanted to go for a screen test, but this was impossible if she was married. Just as easily as she

One of the famous bathing-suit shots

Marilyn married Joe diMaggio in January 1954

had earlier arranged a wedding, Grace arranged a divorce. Norma was sent to Las Vegas and Jim was sent a witness statement. By September their marriage was dissolved and Norma was on her way to the movies.

In July 1946 Norma Jeane arrived at the screen-testing office of Twentieth-Century Fox. Apparently nervous and stuttering, Norma was given a series of simple tasks to perform. The situation looked less than promising but, as the cameras started rolling, Norma Jeane was transformed. Poised, confident, sexy, she was a natural actress and a contract was drawn up. She would be paid $75 a week for six months whether she worked or not. There was just one problem left to solve: no-one, she was told, would know how to pronounce 'Dougherty'. Norma Jeane did not hesitate – she chose 'Monroe', her mother's name and her only indisputable family connection. But Norma Jeane's first name then became problematic since it didn't sound right with the new surname. Her interviewer, Ben Lyon, apparently thinking of a former girlfriend whom Norma Jeane resembled, just leaned forwards and said, 'you're Marilyn'.

But success wasn't to come that easily. Darryl F. Zanuck, the studio's leading producer, treated his staff as chattels to be disposed of at will, and, though his successes were many, he scarcely noticed Marilyn Monroe. The year ended without a single job for the contract actress and though, in February, her contract was renewed for six months, she could still only land a role, her first, as a high school girl in a film memorably entitled *Scudda-Hoo! Scudda-Hay!* Her only words on camera were 'Hi, Rad!' She was considered excess to requirements and, in August 1947, her contract was not renewed. She spent the rest of 1947, like any other small-time actress, hanging around at as many producers' parties as she could and, at one of these, she struck lucky. She met and bedded a friend of Harry Cohn, head of Columbia Studios. He got her an audition with Harry, who offered her a six-month contract. Marilyn moved into the Studio Club, a residential hostel for young actresses, and she considered herself happy.

On New Year's Eve, she was introduced to Johnny Hyde, executive vice-president of the William Morris Agency and, before the night was over, he had fallen madly in love. They began an affair – Marilyn at the time being twenty-two and Johnny Hyde fifty-three. Though married with children, Johnny was desperate to wed Marilyn and he bought out her contract and began devoting his entire professional and personal time to her. He left his family and urged her to live with him. Marilyn, realizing that this would do little to advance her career, continued to sleep with him but maintained her room at the Studio Club. Besotted, he called in all the favours he could muster, and the Marx Brothers incorporated a cameo for his beloved in a film called *Love Happy*. She had nothing to do except look attractive, at which she was very good, and, for a single afternoon, she was paid $500. She was then sent on a nationwide tour to promote the film and was, by all accounts, a media success. But still she got no more serious work.

Johnny Hyde dragged her to MGM to audition for the part of Angela in *The Asphalt Jungle*, directed by the young John Huston. He didn't want her in his picture but Johnny Hyde was a hard man to shake off and, eventually, the director caved in. Marilyn received a few reviews for her appearance but no more work and, after a few minor roles in forgotten pictures, Johnny next took her to try for a small role in a film called *All About Eve*. She did exactly what was required of her but Johnny's hopes were, again, dashed. She got the part but no long-term contract, and the studios still paid her scant attention. Things weren't looking good for Marilyn and, on 18 December 1950, Johnny Hyde died of a massive heart attack, and his wife and children would not permit Marilyn to come to the funeral. She dressed up as a servant and went anyway and, for a while afterwards, was inconsolable. She must have thought that she had lost both the person who loved her most and her best chance of success.

On the set of *As Young as You Feel* a few months later, Marilyn met both Elia Kazan, the director, and Arthur Miller, the playwright. Kazan was married and forty-two. He considered Marilyn to be a simple but attractive girl and the two immediately began an affair, though Marilyn chattered on endlessly in bed about her greater admiration for his friend, Arthur. After Johnny's death, there was little point staying at the William Morris Agency, and she moved to Famous Artists who, almost immediately, secured her a seven-year contract with Fox. Both Kazan and Miller left for New York, and Marilyn began a short correspondence with Arthur, who was at that time married.

Meanwhile, extraordinarily, fan mail began to pour into the Fox studio at a rate of two to three thousand letters each week – more even than for Betty Grable or Gregory Peck. The army newspaper proclaimed her 'Miss Cheesecake of

1951' and, by the end of that year, the studio shareholders were insistent that Marilyn should actually star in a picture. It was eventually not a lover but popular pressure which swayed the studio. The film they chose, and one in which she played a psychopathic baby-sitter, was called *Don't Bother to Knock*.

This was rapidly followed by *Monkey Business* and a personal request to meet her from one of America's baseball legends – Joe diMaggio. He was thirty-seven and divorced; she was twenty-five. He was retired from baseball and had become America's highest paid sports-show host. Though he had never been to a film-set and she had never been to a baseball game, they began an affair early in 1952.

In April, she appeared on the cover of *Life* magazine and was rapidly becoming the most publicised woman of the year. On 1 June, she turned twenty-six, and was looking forward to appearing in a Technicolor thriller called *Niagara*. It was then announced that she would have the second role in a new film called *Gentlemen Prefer Blondes*. Though this was planned for Betty Grable, Marilyn came at half the price. She began to appear at promotional and fund-raising events in increasingly more daring clothing, creating a name for herself as a somewhat sensational self-publicist and sex symbol. Joe diMaggio, who was a good Catholic man, was not pleased. She was seen shopping in New York and was reported by sales assistants to wear no underwear. Everything Marilyn did was becoming news. For *Gentlemen Prefer Blondes*, Marilyn was paid $15,000, and Jane Russell, her co-star, $150,000. The film included the song which was to become her theme tune, 'Diamonds are a Girl's Best Friend' and, surrounded by dozens of men in black tie, Marilyn shimmied her way through the glamour. Her image as a dizzy blonde was now firmly fixed in the public mind.

Early in 1953, Marilyn and Joe made a pact. She would wear less revealing dresses and he would be more understanding of her career. Almost immediately after giving this promise, she was invited to an awards ceremony at which she wore a dress from the film that she

The screen goddess

The famous publicity stunt for *Seven Year Itch*

actually had to be sewn into. The designer begged her not to wear it, claiming that she was too fat, but she was adamant that she would do so. She had discovered a fabulous way to lose weight instantly – colonic irrigation – and she had two sessions that very day, stealing the show from such luminaries as Joan Crawford and Lana Turner. On 26 June, Monroe and Russell placed their hands and feet into wet cement on the forecourt of the Chinese Theater on Hollywood Boulevard, and Marilyn knew that she had at last become a star.

Whilst one life blossomed, another faded: on 1 October, Grace McKee Goddard was buried and Marilyn chose not to go to the funeral. With her increasing success, Marilyn withdrew further and further from her former life. She tried to claim, until proved wrong, that her mother was dead, and she cut off all ties with Grace, who became an alcoholic and subsequently took an overdose. By her twenty-seventh birthday, all of Marilyn's early female role-models had died, except her mother.

Marilyn Monroe's film career spanned sixteen years. During the first eight, she appeared in twenty-four productions; but from 1955 to 1962, in only five. In January 1954, she was suspended by Fox for failing to appear in what would have been the first of these five. Her lawyer told the press that she was fighting for the right to read and chose her scripts for herself but, in fact, she was considerably more bothered by the fixed salary clause in her contract. On 14 January, instead of appearing on the set of *Pink Tights*, she flew to San Francisco where she, at last, married Joe diMaggio. He was thirty-nine; she claimed to be twenty-five (in fact she was twenty-eight). She held three orchids and asked him to promise, if she died before he did, to put flowers on her grave every week. Joe promised and, as the couple came out of the registry office, they were swamped by reporters. Joe spent much of the next few days fulfilling his life's passion – watching television – and on 29 January the couple prepared to fly to Tokyo, where Joe had agreed to do a sports programme on TV. Marilyn hid an apparently bruised hand behind a mink coat and claimed to have bumped it. Later she would refer to Joe as 'my Slugger' – and she'd still never been to a baseball match.

The Japan trip was a triumph for Marilyn and a disaster for Joe. Everywhere they went for his press conferences, she was inundated with questions and fans swarmed about her. He remained in Tokyo whilst Marilyn was given special clearance to go and sing for the troops in Korea. Joe was adamantly opposed to this idea, but she went anyway. For four days, she sang to over 100,000 soldiers and they loved it. It was her first experience with a live audience and it went down a treat. Marilyn felt that she had somewhere she belonged and it wasn't with her new husband. By the time they returned to San Francisco at the end of

Marilyn with Arthur Miller

With Jack Lemmon in *Some Like it Hot*

February, Marilyn was ready to receive her award for best performances of 1953, but her husband would not accompany her to the ceremony. Her old friend, Sidney Skolsky, went with her instead and, that evening in the hotel, she stunned him by announcing that she was now going to marry Arthur Miller.

Marilyn started work on *The Seven Year Itch* and her appearance on set was increasingly beset by lateness and drowsiness. She had begun to take barbiturates and her marriage was clearly on the rocks. She almost certainly began an affair with her dance coach, Hal Schaefer, and when she tried to call it off, he took an overdose. Marilyn was nervous and touchy. On set she fell over and, as she regained her composure, she was introduced to a family who were to take on enormous importance in her life – the Strasbergs. She already knew who they were and Lee's work as a drama coach had been recommended to her by, amongst others, Elia Kazan and Marlon Brando. Paula, his wife, and Susan, his daughter, asked her to New York, an invitation that Marilyn was to take very seriously indeed.

In September, Marilyn flew to Manhattan for the famous publicity stunt that was to bring *The Seven Year Itch* to front pages around the world. Everyone knew that the photographs would have to be retaken at the studio but, for over two hours, the star stood in the middle of Lexington Avenue as thousands of members of the public watched her specially designed dress fly high over her waist to reveal nothing but a pair of white knickers. The scenes in the street were sensational. The public had never seen anything like it. But they had one dire consequence. The previous evening, Joe had received a call from an old friend who urged him to come to New York. As soon as he arrived, Joe was hustled to Lexington Avenue, against his own wishes, in order to see the goings-on for himself. As his wife's skirt flew high into the air, Joe turned to the director of the film, Billy Wilder, with 'the look of death' on his face and, later that night, screams were heard from the couple's hotel bedroom. Marilyn's make-up artist covered up the bruises all over her body. Two weeks later, Marilyn filed for divorce.

The Pressures Mount

Marilyn's inability to arrive on set on time became chronic. Billy Wilder was sympathetic, knowing that the film's success depended largely on his star, but she was on ever-increasing doses of sleeping pills and her marriage was a disaster. She apologized to her co-star, Tom Ewell, for the smell of medicine on her breath during the kissing scenes and, though Marilyn and Joe continued to share the same house, Joe was handed a divorce petition. Movie cameras set up outside their home as the most photographed couple in America moved around inside. The separation was world news. Joe left in a Cadillac for San Francisco, and Marilyn appeared on the set of *Seven Year Itch* the next morning, saying that she felt alive for the first time in days. On 27 October, in less than eight minutes, they were divorced. On 4 November the film was finished and the studio gave a gala dinner in her honour at which she danced with Clark Gable and drank with Humphrey Bogart. She had never felt so popular or so accepted by Hollywood society.

Later that year she had a minor gynaecological operation and Joe was by her side again, leading to rumours of a reconciliation. Marilyn denied that this was true, but her ex-husband was clearly still devoted to her and the pair would always be friends. For Christmas 1954, Marilyn travelled to New York to stay with her old friends, the Greenes. Joe diMaggio came to visit her constantly, though it's very likely that she was having an affair with Milton Greene throughout this period. It was he who leased a suite for her in New York and, through the introduction of Elia Kazan, she at last enrolled for classes at Lee Strasberg's famous Actors Studio.

He was fifty-four and had started the legendary drama school in 1931. There were no formal classes, and attendance was at the invitation of Lee himself. 'We were like converts to a new religion,'

With Clark Gable in *The Misfits*

Looking lost in *Something's Got to Give*

said Eli Wallach. 'We all thought we would do Shakespeare and marry each other,' said Shelley Winters. His method followed the principle that every performance is based on one's unique personality. He emphasized true emotion based on personal experience and thus became a kind of analyst-doctor to his students. 'You learn to dig into your unconscious,' said Marlon Brando, a leading ex-pupil. With such high-profile students, the method was, naturally, fabulously fashionable.

Marilyn, said Lee, merely had to open up her unconscious and, to do so, she would have to enter psychoanalysis. She began a course of therapy with Milton Greene's own analyst, Margaret Hohenberg, and she toured the streets of

New York wearing jeans and no make-up. She continued with her classes and was introduced to some new friends, a poet and his wife, Mr and Mrs Rosten. They, in turn, were college friends of Arthur Miller, so the reintroduction, for which Marilyn had waited so long, was negotiated.

Miller would turn forty that year and Marilyn was twenty-nine. His marriage was, by this stage, in some difficulties and, since last seeing Marilyn, he had had a massive success with *The Crucible* and *A View from the Bridge* was about to open.

'She was simply overwhelming,' he would later say. 'She had so much promise . . . there wasn't a conventional bone in her body.' Marilyn, however, wasn't at all sure that she wanted to marry Arthur and this made him all the more keen. He was also in the first throes of being hounded as a Communist sympathizer. Marilyn, whilst searching for her inner self, often went shopping in disguise. Then she grew agitated at the lack of public recognition and, on one occasion, deliberately removed her disguise in the middle of New York's leading department store. She often stayed overnight at the Strasbergs' home, generally receiving far more attention than their own two children.

On 1 June, she attended the première of *The Seven Year Itch* along with Grace Kelly, Henry Fonda and Eddie Fisher.

The film was the summer's biggest grosser, and Marilyn, the most photographed person in America. There was a fifty-two-foot high poster of her erected on Broadway, and Joe diMaggio accompanied her to the première. At the same time, she continued to date Arthur Miller and stayed at the Strasbergs' as often as four times a week. The sleeping pills she took with ever-increasing frequency became less and less effective and her dating of Arthur Miller meant that the FBI opened a file on her and every move she made was carefully monitored in case she was secretly a Russian spy.

She returned to Hollywood to film *Bus Stop*, accompanied by the Greenes. With Paula Strasberg, Marilyn ran through every line of *Bus Stop*, analysing and re-analysing and, when filming started, Paula was to be on set at all times. 'Marilyn is too weak to be able to handle this alone,' said Lee, and Paula was thus paid more than any other member of the crew and deeply resented by all.

By June, filming was finished and Marilyn went to New York to join Arthur Miller and to be near him whilst he attended the House Un-American Activities hearings in Washington DC. He was charged with being a Communist sympathizer and he could have gone to jail. Marilyn, with her abiding interest in underdogs and vague notions of civil liberties, was proud of him and, during the hearing, on national television, Miller announced that he needed his passport in order to travel to England that summer and be with his new wife.

The news was sensational and the couple promised to meet the press in Connecticut on 29 June whilst a fanatical crowd of reporters and fans began to gather. On the way to the registry office, the couple merely wanted to be left in peace. One photographer's car, however, managed to follow them and, in the rush, went hurtling around a corner and crashed. The occupant, a former Russian princess, was instantaneously killed and Marilyn considered the incident to be a bad omen. The wedding took place that afternoon. One of the guests quipped, 'I hope your children have Arthur's looks and Marilyn's brains.'

Marilyn was rumoured to be involved with
John F Kennedy

Marilyn's house outside Hollywood

On 13 July the couple, along with Marilyn's whole entourage, travelled to London. Everywhere she went, Marilyn was mobbed, and the Millers set up home in Parkside House in Egham, near Windsor Park. Filming was immediately beset with problems. Paula Strasberg immediately decided that she was the most important person on the set, and Marilyn began to take large doses of sleeping pills to cover her increasing anxiety and insecurity. Arthur Miller clearly resented the huge influence of the Strasbergs, and Lee was banned from the set: but Marilyn couldn't function without the presence of Paula, and so her presence had to be tolerated.

Still, Marilyn was a huge hit in England and was to meet the Queen at a royal gala première. Other guests at the screening included Brigitte Bardot and Joan Crawford but Marilyn was undoubtedly the star and the press loved her, though rumours abounded about her drug dependency and her lateness on set. Still, by November the film was finished and the Millers returned to New York. Marilyn tried to assume the role of housewife and she bought a flat at 444 East 57th Street which she immediately spent most of her time redecorating.

Marilyn began daily counselling with an entirely new therapist and, each day, after her therapy session, she immediately took the lift and went for another hour's session with Lee Strasberg, who just happened to live in the same building. More and more people were vying for ultimate control of the living icon. Miller naturally resented all of this outside interference and the couple grew estranged. Marilyn was prone to outbursts of crying and the Strasbergs and Miller grew to hate each other openly, both blaming the other for her condition. Marilyn began to put on weight and, in May 1957, Arthur was found guilty on two counts of failing to answer HUAC in 1956. An appeal was lodged, but this was another blow to the couple's simple desire for a peaceful existence.

They spent the summer at their beachhouse at Amagansett on Long Island and Arthur began writing the screenplay of *The Misfits*, especially for Marilyn. Marilyn cried at almost anything and the couple rarely spoke. But it was just at this time that she was sent a two-page outline by Billy Wilder of a script he was working on with I.A.L.Diamond. It was called *Some Like It Hot*. Marilyn considered it a suitable stopgap while she waited for Arthur to finish *The Misfits*, and in July she returned to Los Angeles to begin work on what was to become her most famous film.

Very quickly, the early good spirits on set turned sour. Jack Lemmon and Tony Curtis grew increasingly irritated as Marilyn required ten to fifteen takes of each shot. One scene would often take as long as three days whilst Marilyn forgot her lines, began to cry, and had her make-up reapplied. She constantly arrived late and, though a year younger

Lee Strasberg at Marilyn's funeral

A Marilyn memorabilia shop

than Curtis and Lemmon, Marilyn was convinced that she looked older. Curtis famously claimed that kissing Marilyn was like kissing Hitler, and Marilyn was considered by the whole crew to be a pain in the ass, which did nothing to relieve her many insecurities. She began to take pills in the afternoons as well as at night, and Wilder thought that the picture would never be finished. Arthur arrived to help, but he only made things worse. She felt that he considered her inadequate, and the rest of the crew were merely embarrassed by such obvious lack of mutual respect. Wilder said, 'I have discussed this project with my doctor and my psychiatrist, and they tell me I'm too old and too rich to go through this again.'

The film, of course, became one of the most celebrated ever made and the biggest grossing film for 1959 but, by December, Marilyn's diet consisted of amytal, nembutal and daily enemas. After a quiet summer, Marilyn received the script of *Let's Make Love* and, unfortunately, considered it full of promise. By this time her reputation was so appalling that Cary Grant, Rock Hudson and Charlton Heston, amongst others, all turned down the opportunity to be her leading man. A solution was found in the form of Yves Montand, who was a massive star in Europe but had never played in an English-language film. He was thrilled at any opportunity to do so.

In January the Millers were installed in bungalow number 20 at the Beverly

Hills Hotel, and Yves Montand and his wife, Simone Signoret, were lodged next door. The couples dined together often and then Miller went to Ireland to work with John Huston on a new draft of *The Misfits*. By spring, the problems on set seemed insurmountable. Yves realized that his role was nothing but a useless foil to Marilyn's, and she was panic-stricken about her performance. Simone Signoret returned to France and Yves appeared, almost immediately, in Marilyn's bungalow in order to comfort her in her solitude.

'I bent over to kiss her good-night, but suddenly it was a wild kiss, a fire, a hurricane I couldn't stop,' he said. But, by June, filming was finished and

Yves, too, returned to his wife in France. Even Paula Strasberg left to visit her daughter. Marilyn, in despair, turned to yet another therapist, Dr Ralph Greenson, and this time she went to therapy seven days a week. He also, unwisely, supplied her with plentiful and constant barbiturates.

In July 1960, Marilyn set off for Nevada to begin filming *The Misfits* – a tale of cowboys and a divorced woman, much of which Miller drew from both his own divorce and his experience of Marilyn. She naturally resented what she felt was an intrusion; but at last she got to work with her hero, Clark Gable, though she was in agony, unable to digest food and violently sick every morning.

Arthur rewrote pages of script every evening and, though they now slept in separate bungalows, this made Marilyn's inability to remember lines even more pitiable. Pills were flown in from LA every other day and she was now on three times the recommended dosage of most drugs. Her speech was incoherent. She was so drowsy in the mornings that she often had her make-up applied while still in bed. Marilyn was required to return to LA for a function, where she collapsed and was taken to hospital, which was fortunate since the wildly over-budget picture had now run out of cash.

Eventually, by November, the film was finished. Marilyn and Arthur prepared to announce their divorce and Marilyn had completed her last finished film. A few days later, she heard that Clark Gable had had a heart attack and was dead. She returned to New York and she spent Christmas 1960 with the Strasbergs, her only remaining allies.

A Desperate Year

Considering that this would lessen publicity, Marilyn divorced Arthur on 20 January 1961, the same day as Kennedy's inauguration, and she promptly made a new will, leaving 75 per cent of her estate to Lee Strasberg. *The Misfits* was a critical disappointment and Marilyn grew depressed and stayed in her darkened bedroom, listening to sentimental records and losing weight. Her New York therapist grew concerned and drove Marilyn to the New York Hospital complex, where she was placed in the psychiatric ward in a locked and padded room. She was pitched into a state of extreme shock and considered that she had, at last, inherited the disease of her ancestors. She broke down, weeping and sobbing, and she banged on the locked steel door. Staff reaction concluded that she was indeed a psychiatric case and she was ignored. After two days and nights, she was in a state of hysteria and smuggled out a note to the Strasbergs, begging for help. They did nothing. In desperation, Marilyn contacted Joe diMaggio, whom she had not seen for six years but who had never remarried and who was still madly in love with her.

He arrived the very next evening from Florida and demanded that Marilyn be released or he would take the hospital apart brick by brick. The therapist, trembling with remorse, repeated over and over, 'I did a terrible thing'. This admission did not help her, however, since she was dismissed the next day and never saw Marilyn again. Marilyn agreed to enter a private rest-home if Joe would stay with her every day, which he did, and she remained recuperating until March.

She then went with Joe to Florida, where she relaxed and swam. Marilyn thrilled the Yankees baseball team, whom Joe was coaching at the time, by appearing at a match and cheering them on. In April she returned to Los

Angeles and, by June, she was clearly well enough to have started an intermittent affair with Frank Sinatra.

Marilyn resumed her sessions with Dr Greenson and, despite a brief reappearance and reunion with her half-sister Berniece, Dr Greenson considered that outside influences were malevolent and began to order Marilyn to send away all of her remaining entourage, including anyone who disagreed with him. It was suggested that she play in a film called *Something's Got to Give*, whose script she did not like, but Dr Greenson considered it a good idea so she took on the role. He ordered her to buy a house, which she did, and then he ordered her to take on a strange woman called Eunice Murray as her housekeeper, and she did this also. Joe arrived for Christmas and they spent the season quietly together.

In October 1961 Marilyn had met John F. Kennedy at a dinner party in his honour. She was one of a number of blonde stars on offer that night – Kim Novak and Angie Dickinson amongst them. She was driven back to her house by the host's staff and, in February 1962, she met the President again when she went to a dinner party in New York but, on this occasion too, she was escorted home. Though Marilyn also met John's brother, Robert Kennedy, four times, there is no real evidence that these two had an affair. She did ring him on more than one occasion to ask him questions about civil rights, but this apparently annoyed more than attracted him, and that seems to have been it.

On 2 March, Marilyn went to an awards dinner, apparently 'drunk, barely in control, her voice slurred'. She had received potent injections of nembutal, seconal and phenobarbital, and Greenson simultaneously gave her even heavier doses of sleeping pills. She didn't know if *Something's Got to Give* would ever be made and she was a nervous wreck. She collapsed at Greenson's home and Joe diMaggio arrived to see her. Greenson forbade him entry but Joe, once again, managed to rescue her and bring her home. It was at this stage that she met JFK for the third time. This occurred on 24 March 1962 when the two were both house guests of Bing

Crosby in Palm Springs. On that occasion they definitely shared a bedroom, and Marilyn telephoned her masseur from the room and asked his advice about muscle tension. Marilyn always claimed that this was the only weekend they ever spent in bed together, despite the numerous rumours to the contrary, and, certainly, the only evidence of a fourth meeting was at the legendary birthday gala in his benefit in New York. Her daily activities developed into a routine which began with a facial, continued with a session with Greenson and went on with a script-reading session with Paula Strasberg. Marilyn would then go for her daily injection of barbiturates, do some shopping and return for an afternoon session with Greenson. The schedule was only broken by occasional fittings and make-up tests.

On 30 April she appeared for the first time on the set of *Something's Got to Give* and then she returned home and collapsed in bed. She stayed in bed, sick, day after day and then announced her intention to appear at JFK's birthday gala. Marilyn submitted to hours of fittings for her dress, which would be a sheer body-stocking embroidered with sequins and with nothing underneath. Filming continued without the presence of Marilyn, whose behaviour became increasingly erratic. Greenson went on a five-week foreign tour and left Marilyn with a potentially lethal supply of a drug called dexamyl, which is now banned. Joe came to stay and Marilyn, temporarily free of her tyrant, managed to dismiss Greenson's spy, Mrs Murray, at last. She perked up enough to appear on set for three days in a row, but this was not enough. As Marilyn flew to New York for JFK's birthday, she was in the process of being fired.

On 19 May, at Madison Square Gardens, Jack Benny introduced the acts – Ella Fitzgerald and Maria Callas amongst them. The benefit, in aid of the Democratic Party, was in honour of the President's forty-fifth birthday. As usual, Marilyn was late, and Peter Lawford was told to introduce her in just this way: 'Mr President – the late Marilyn Monroe'. A nervous Marilyn began to sing 'Happy Birthday' whilst the audience cheered and shouted. Marilyn's guest, typically, was Isadore Miller, Arthur's father, and, at the party afterwards, her main concern was that he should have a chair and a plate of food. She just wanted someone steady to love.

The following day, she returned to Los Angeles where Mrs Murray had ignored her notice of dismissal and simply re-appeared. Marilyn carried on filming *Something's Got to Give* as though nothing had happened, and she celebrated her thirty-sixth birthday. No one turned up for her party and she spent most of the evening alone. It was all too much for her and she attempted to take an overdose. Greenson came rushing back from Europe to be her saviour. The film was, meanwhile, in the last throes of despair, though Greenson said he was willing to stand in and assume responsibility for all creative areas of the picture, including the selection of a new director and cameraman. Since he was a psychotherapist and knew nothing of films, this was merely an expression of egomania. Dean Martin, the co-star, however, said he would refuse to act with anyone else and Marilyn was touched to tears. Negotiations were resumed for recommencement in the autumn and Greenson's daily sessions and injections continued.

In July, Joe diMaggio once again arrived to rescue her and announced that he would be giving up his work at the end of the month. Marilyn gave what was to be her last interview: 'Please,' she said in a whisper, 'please don't make me a joke.'

Marilyn and Joe decided to remarry and set a date of 8 August. Older and wiser now, they thought that this time they could do better. Marilyn was re-signed for *Something's Got to Give* and things were really looking up. On 1 August she eventually sacked Mrs Murray for good – the old bat would leave the day after the wedding. Marilyn spent the next few days organizing for this happy event.

On 4 August, Greenson came and spent the day with her, giving her large doses of injections. At 7.30 Joe diMaggio jun rang and had a perfectly pleasant conversation with Marilyn but, by 7.45, when Peter Lawford rang to invite Marilyn to dinner, she was incoherent and only able to mumble, 'Goodbye, goodbye'. Peter was desperately concerned and wanted to go round straight away, but his friends urged him not to – he was JFK's brother-in-law and not in a position to encourage negative publicity. Lawford persisted in ordering that someone else go and check up on the star, but it was already too late. By midnight, news had spread that she was dead. Though Greenson and Murray swore they had to break down doors and smash windows to get into Marilyn's bedroom when they suspected something was wrong, this cannot be true. From the day she had been incarcerated in New York Hospital, Marilyn had never locked a door. There were no locks in the entire house. Though no one can ever know what actually happened that night, all that can be said for sure is that both of these witnesses clearly told lies at the inquest.

The police were not informed for over four hours. There was no suicide note, and Marilyn was found, stark naked, lying on her bed. There were no signs of external violence or bruising. The only highly unusual symptom was severe and recent bruising of the colon – leading to the conclusion that a fatal dose of drugs was ingested by means of an enema. It is virtually incredible that anyone could apply such an anti-medication on themselves. The identity of the person who did apply it remains a secret to this day. And, for the rest of his life, Joe diMaggio laid flowers at the grave of his beloved each and every week, just as he had promised. He never remarried.